Handling the Word of Truth

Learn how to study and teach the Bible

*Be diligent to present yourself approved to God as a
workman who does not need to be ashamed,
handling accurately the word of truth.*
2 Timothy 2:15

Rob Dingman

*line
upon
line*

Handling Accurately the Word of Truth

© 2016 Rob Dingman
All rights reserved.

ISBN 978-0-9571329-3-1

Published by Line Upon Line
www.calvarychapeltwickenham.com

Designed by Hand-Maid Design, London

Set in Adobe Jensen Pro
with chapter heads in Myriad Pro

To those who taught me so much,
and all the people I have learned from
while I have been teaching them
to study and teach the Bible

Contents

Introduction

This book is a primer in learning how to study and teach the Bible. It's a starting point. A pastor who tried this out on his men told me that it didn't intimidate them. I took that as a compliment. May this encourage you to learn to study and teach the Bible.

I originally wrote this very quickly to send to a pastors' conference in Uganda that I was not able to attend for health reasons. It was a short print run, soon gone. Other people have read it and asked me to make it more available. My thanks to those who have encouraged me.

Jesus commanded us to pray that the Lord of the harvest send out labourers into His harvest. This book can help you become prepared to be a labourer. Pastors, give this to the men that you want to encourage into ministry.

We will cover the workflow of teaching. It starts with study: how to observe the text of the Bible, how to interpret it, and how to apply it to make it practical. Then we look at how to turn the results of study into a message. Finally, we look at how to prepare your life to teach. A Bible teacher has to live out his teaching. Our lives either confirm the truth of the Bible or contradict it. We must develop our character as much as our ability to study and teach.

What I want to give you I also received from many people. If you receive from this book you should in turn pass this knowledge on to others. May God bless you greatly as you receive from Him.

Rob Dingman
Pastor
Calvary Chapel Twickenham
London, England

1. Causing the people to get the sense

This chapter is an introduction to a way of teaching that will result in people coming to know Jesus Christ and the message of the Bible. This method is to teach through the whole Bible, teaching through whole books of the Bible, chapter by chapter, verse by verse.

The purpose is to give the sense of what is being said in the Bible passage, to show the principles being taught, and to make the principles apply practically to everyday life.

That is what is happening in Nehemiah chapter 8. We will teach in the same way that Ezra and the other Levites do as they demonstrate this idea.

1 Now all the people gathered together as one man in the open square that was in front of the Water Gate; and they told Ezra the scribe to bring the Book of the Law of Moses, which the LORD had commanded Israel. 2 So Ezra the priest brought the Law before the assembly of men and women and all who could hear with understanding on the first day of the seventh month. 3 Then he read from it in the open square that was in front of the Water Gate from morning until midday, before the men and women and those who could understand; and the ears of all the people were attentive to the Book of the Law.

4 So Ezra the scribe stood on a platform of wood which they had made for the purpose; and beside him, at his right hand, stood Mattithiah, Shema, Anaiah, Urijah, Hilkiah, and Maaseiah; and at his left hand Pedaiah, Mishael, Malchijah, Hashum, Hashbadana, Zechariah, and Meshullam.

5 And Ezra opened the book in the sight of all the people, for he was standing above all the people; and when he opened it, all the people stood up.

6 And Ezra blessed the LORD, the great God. Then all the people answered, "Amen, Amen!" while lifting up their hands. And they bowed their heads and worshiped the LORD with their faces to the ground.

7 Also Jeshua, Bani, Sherebiah, Jamin, Akkub, Shabbethai, Hodijah, Maaseiah, Kelita, Azariah, Jozabad, Hanan, Pelaiah, and the Levites, helped the people to understand the Law; and the people stood in their place.

8 So they read distinctly from the book, in the Law of God; and they gave the sense, and helped them to understand the reading.

9 And Nehemiah, who was the governor, Ezra the priest and scribe, and the Levites who taught the people said to all the people, "This day is holy to the LORD your God; do not mourn nor weep." For all the people wept, when they heard the words of the Law.

10 Then he said to them, "Go your way, eat the fat, drink the sweet, and send portions to those for whom nothing is prepared; for this day is holy to our LORD. Do not sorrow, for the joy of the LORD is your strength."

11 So the Levites quieted all the people, saying, "Be still, for the day is holy; do not be grieved."

12 And all the people went their way to eat and drink, to send portions and rejoice greatly, because they understood the words that were declared to them.

The Word of God is important to Israel

In verse 1, Ezra the scribe is asked to bring the Book of the Law which the Lord had given to Israel through Moses.

This is extremely important in the life of Israel. God greatly punished Israel and sent them to Babylon because they disobeyed His law. They had to live seventy years away from the land God gave them.

Now they were shown mercy by God and brought back into the land, but their ability to stay there depended on their obedience to God. The law promised that if they disobeyed God, they would again be punished and sent out of the land.

Moses taught the importance of the Word of God in Deuteronomy 32:45–47:

> Moses finished speaking all these words to all Israel, and He said to them: "Set your hearts on all the words which I testify among you today, which you shall command your children to be careful to observe—all the words of this law. For it is not a futile thing for you, because it is your life, and by this word you shall prolong your days in the land which you cross over the Jordan to possess."

Thus, it was important to their very lives that they know the Word of God and obey it.

Who receives the word: all who understand

In verse 2 we notice who received the teaching of the law: those who could hear with understanding. This is repeated in verse 3. It was for those who had minds and hearts to not only hear but understand.

God means for us to understand His Word. He gave us minds so we can think and come to know and understand. The greatest thing we can think of and understand is the Word of God.

I have found that people can understand more of the Bible than we think they can. Once I was asked to teach a Bible study at a drug rehabilitation centre. The director told me to make it short. "They have taken so many drugs that they don't have any attention span at all," he said.

I decided I would teach as long as I had their attention. I was able to give a forty-minute study of Numbers 21:4–9, the account of the bronze serpent in the wilderness. I did that to explain what Jesus meant in John 3:14–15 about His death being like that bronze serpent.

After the study the director told me how amazing it was that they listened to me. He kept saying he couldn't understand how that could have happened! But these accounts in the Bible are interesting and can hold people's attention if we take care to identify the message accurately and deliver it clearly.

The people were attentive

Verse 3 says the ears of all the people were attentive to the Book of the Law. They were not bored or wishing they were somewhere else. They were interested. They were listening with the right attitude in order to receive the knowledge of God and hear teaching about what they were to become as God's people.

We can understand their interest: their lives depended on understanding the law and doing it.

Our lives also depend on knowing the Word of God and doing it. We need to know Jesus as He is in truth and trust in Him according to the Word of God.

Ezra taught on a wooden platform

He stood on a wooden podium that they had built for this purpose. This lifted him up above the people so they could see him and hear him from far away. It was not so Ezra could be the star of the show. The focus was on the Word of God, not any personality.

Many teachers, same message

Notice in verse 4 that there were other men on the podium besides Ezra. There were thirteen other men, six on his right hand, and seven on his left. He wasn't the only teacher. In verse 7, thirteen other men, besides Levites, also explained the Law to the people. The men were surely all different in ages, personalities, and abilities, but they all delivered the same message: the Word of God.

This brings a wonderful humility to teaching. It's not important who is delivering the message; it's important that the message be delivered.

The meeting began and continued with worship

In verse 6 Ezra blessed the Lord, and the people responded. Together they worshipped. Then the teaching of the Word began. Some people think that worship is singing songs, and the teaching is after the worship is over. But realize that the worship did not stop when the bowing down to God ended. Jesus quoted the great commandment in Matthew 22:37, "You shall love the LORD your God with all your heart, with all your soul, and with all your mind." The teaching of the Word of God is directed at our minds and wills and is in itself worship to the Lord.

They read much Scripture, in context

If the people were to obey the law, they had to hear and understand the whole law. It wouldn't help if they heard only bits and pieces and didn't understand the connection between them.

In the first five books of Moses there is more than just law. There is history that explains who the nation of Israel is and how they came to be. They owe their direct existence to God. He created them. He saved them out of Egypt and slavery. He asked if they wanted to be His special people and obey His laws, and they said yes. They made a covenant, so the Lord would be their God and Israel would be His people.

That is the context for these laws. It shows they are not manmade laws, but God-given. These laws are reasonable because of Israel's history with God and the covenant they made. There is a good reason for Israel to obey them.

They let the Word of God speak for itself

1. **They read distinctly from the book.** It is possible to read aloud in a way that gets the words correct, but shows there is no understanding of what is being read. A machine could read the words, but a machine doesn't know anything and can't teach anyone.

The teachers knew what the Scriptures said and what they meant. They read them so that people would get understanding, simply by putting the emphasis on the right words. They read clearly and gave each word its proper emphasis.

2. **The teachers gave the sense.** Moses wrote down the Scriptures one thousand years before Ezra. Culture, language, and customs can change in that much time. In order for the people to understand the Word of God certain ideas and words needed to be clarified. The teachers had to think ahead

and anticipate difficulties. They asked themselves: what would people grasp easily? Where would they need help? Then they explained difficult parts in the Scriptures.

They translated. The Scriptures were written in Hebrew, the language of the Jews. When the people were taken into captivity they had to learn the languages of Babylon. Upon returning to Israel, they continued using those languages and spoke less Hebrew, so many people did not clearly understand all that was written. The teachers had to bring out what was important to know from the original language to help the people to understand.

They defined any words that were no longer in common use. Otherwise they would be meaningless.

They explained customs and ancient things in the Scriptures that were not customs in the present time.

The teachers tried to make Moses understandable one thousand years after his time, so the people would hear Moses speaking directly to them.

3. They helped them understand the reading. All the work the teachers did was for this one thing: that the people would understand the reading. Once they understood, they would have the possibility to know right from wrong, and choose to do right. Then they would avoid evil and be able to stay in the land because they were pleasing to God.

God wants ordinary people to understand the Scriptures and know God for themselves.

4. They helped the people apply the teaching. The Word of God is given to change our lives. This happens as we first understand it and then apply it practically. James 1:22 tells us to not just be hearers of the word but doers. After we make clear what the Word says, then we make it practical. We ask the questions, "What happens if I do what this says? What happens if I don't do it? What will happen then?"

Failure in the light of the Law

The people's reaction showed they had been listening. They wept and mourned, feeling conviction because of their sin and the sin of their fathers. They could see their disobedience: that they fell short of the glory of God. The people decided that, from what they heard, they were under the condemnation of God. They knew they deserved punishment. It is no surprise that they felt condemned.

The teachers correct the application

What was the teachers' goal in communicating the meaning of the Law? Did they want to make the people feel bad and sorry for their sins? No. They wanted the people to understand the Law so they would not be exiled out of the land a second time and scattered among the nations. The teachers realised the people were making a wrong application of the teaching.

They had to go further and teach that this day was holy to the Lord. It was a day of forgiveness and restoration. The teaching of the Law was not to condemn the people, but so they would know the Law, practice it, and be close to God. They were to share the holiness of God and be His people. Because they would share His holiness, they would also share His joy. The joy of being with God would be their strength.

If the people do not find their happiness in the Lord, they will look elsewhere for satisfaction. They will look at other gods who promise happiness but deceive their followers and cause them to be judged by the Lord.

But if they became happy in the Lord, they would not look elsewhere for satisfaction and happiness. Then they would obey God, be happy, and stay in the land. In this way Nehemiah, Ezra, and the Levites calmed the people from their mourning.

Now the people rejoice greatly

Once the people heard the complete message of God (God is holy, obey His Law, and be His people) and the right application (therefore, walk with Him and be holy and happy), they understood the whole message of God. They became truly happy. They ate and drank and shared with one another.

Application

Now we want to draw some practical principles from what we learn in Nehemiah 8.

1. The church needs the whole counsel of God. Just as Israel needed to live in right relationship with God, so do the people in our churches. They need to know God and walk with Him in holiness. They can only do this through the Word of God.

Paul said in Acts 20:27, "For I have not shunned to declare to you the whole counsel of God."

He wrote in 2 Timothy 3:16–4:2:

> All Scripture is given by inspiration of God, and is profitable for doctrine, for reproof, for correction, for instruction in righteousness, that the man of God may be complete, thoroughly equipped for every good work. I charge you therefore before God and the Lord Jesus Christ, who will judge the living and the dead at His appearing and His kingdom: Preach the word!

We need the whole Bible. We need the account of Creation; we need all the history; we need the Psalms, the covenants,

17

and the promises. They are the foundation for the New Testament, the fulfilment of all the promises and covenants.

> Then He said to them, "These are the words which I spoke to you while I was still with you, that all things must be fulfilled which were written in the Law of Moses and the Prophets and the Psalms concerning Me." And He opened their understanding, that they might comprehend the Scriptures. Luke 24:44–45

2. People will live or die by this Word. Moses said in Deuteronomy 32:46–47,

> "Set your hearts on all the words which I testify among you today, which you shall command your children to be careful to observe—all the words of this law. For it is not a futile thing for you, because it is your life, and by this word you shall prolong your days in the land which you cross over the Jordan to possess."

Just as Israel's life depended on knowing and keeping the Word of God, every single person's life depends on knowing and keeping the Word of God.

Jesus quoted this to the devil: "It is written, 'Man shall not live by bread alone, but by every word that proceeds from the mouth of God'" (Matthew 4:4).

3. The Word has the power to convict of sin. A day of reading the Word of God convinced Israel that they were sinners. And we need this power to convince of sin. Unless people are convinced that they are sinners they won't see the need for a Saviour. Jesus said in John 16:8,

> "And when He (the Holy Spirit) has come, He will convict the world of sin, and of righteousness, and of judgement."

The Holy Spirit will use the Word of God to do His work.

4. The Word has the power to make joyful. Hearing about the grace of God made the people joyful because they knew they were right with God. The Word of God convinces people of two things: that they are sinners and that the only way to be saved is through Jesus.

> So then faith comes by hearing, and hearing by the word of God. Romans 10:17

5. People will be able to understand it. After the Levites taught, the people showed they could understand it. It wasn't complicated; it didn't confuse them. They understood too well about condemnation. They also understood God's mercy and forgiveness.

In the same way our people will understand when we teach them all of what God says in the Bible. They will also be happy!

6. A pastor's job is to deliver the message. Pastors do not have to make up messages. God has given them in the Bible. Our job is to accurately dig out the message from the Bible, give the sense, explain it, and deliver it accurately. Then the Word will do its work of convincing, convicting, and enabling people to believe it.

I encourage you to teach the Bible book by book, chapter by chapter, and verse by verse. In the next few chapters we will look at how to do that.

2. Why teach the whole Bible?

If you're like me, when you hear about teaching the whole Bible, you probably think to yourself: "That's a big job. It'll be a lot of work. Do I really want to do this?" You must be convinced that it's a good thing to do, worth the commitment and effort you put into it.

Why would we want to teach the Bible in our ministry? Please follow along with me as we read in 2 Timothy 3.

1 But know this, that in the last days perilous times will come:

2 For men will be lovers of themselves, lovers of money, boasters, proud, blasphemers, disobedient to parents, unthankful, unholy,

3 unloving, unforgiving, slanderers, without self-control, brutal, despisers of good,

4 traitors, headstrong, haughty, lovers of pleasure rather than lovers of God,

5 having a form of godliness but denying its power. And from such people turn away!

6 For of this sort are those who creep into households and make captives of gullible women loaded down with sins, led away by various lusts,

7 always learning and never able to come to the knowledge of the truth.

8 Now as Jannes and Jambres resisted Moses, so do these also resist the truth: men of corrupt minds, disapproved concerning the faith;

9 but they will progress no further, for their folly will be manifest to all, as theirs also was.

10 But you have carefully followed my doctrine, manner of life, purpose, faith, longsuffering, love, perseverance,

11 persecutions, afflictions, which happened to me at Antioch, at Iconium, at Lystra—what persecutions I endured. And out of them all the Lord delivered me.

12 Yes, and all who desire to live godly in Christ Jesus will suffer persecution.

13 But evil men and impostors will grow worse and worse, deceiving and being deceived.

14 But you must continue in the things which you have learned and been assured of, knowing from whom you have learned them,

15 and that from childhood you have known the Holy Scriptures, which are able to make you wise for salvation through faith which is in Christ Jesus.

16 All Scripture is given by inspiration of God, and is profitable for doctrine, for reproof, for correction, for instruction in righteousness,

17 that the man of God may be complete, thoroughly equipped for every good work.

Perilous times because of perilous men

The word perilous will describe the last days. That means "full of danger". There is a great chance of losing possessions and lives when times are dangerous.

When we look at this list in verses 1–5, we might be tempted to think, "What is so different about the last days? These sins have been around for hundreds and thousands of years! What is so dangerous about the last days?"

The last days are dangerous because Paul is talking about men in the church. They will have a form of godliness but deny its power. Godliness is a power working in a believer's life that makes him change his life to be conformed to Christ. Sin must go. Everything opposed to Christ must surrender. If men deny the power of godliness over them, that means they are not submitted to the lordship of Christ. They don't obey His Word. They look godly from the outside, they might tell others to be godly and teach them so, but they themselves will be no better than unbelievers who are outside the church.

Like unbelievers, they will be lovers of themselves and lovers of pleasure rather than lovers of God. And this will be in the church!

Galatians 5:21 says that those who practice such things will not inherit the kingdom of God.

Captives of lust, never learning the truth

These men will be captives of lust, looking for weak women they can manipulate.

They will be learning, but never come to a definite knowledge of the truth. If a man admits there is truth, the truth rules over the man. But these men will not be ruled by godliness, so they will not be ruled by truth either.

Paul's life is the true standard for Timothy

In verse 10 Paul begins to remind Timothy of all the things he learned and from whom he learned it.

He points out his doctrine, which is his teaching about Jesus, and his understanding of the Scriptures, which he learned from God. His manner of life was to imitate Christ in His serving the Father and living in holiness. His purpose was to know Christ and serve Him. His faith was in Christ and the Scriptures.

He points out the quality of his life that comes from having a true faith. Faith by itself is incomplete without qualities that complement faith: longsuffering, love, perseverance. Men who love themselves do not show any of these qualities, especially that of enduring persecution. No one is persecuted for loving himself, but is persecuted for living selflessly and holy like Jesus Christ.

If godliness sounds difficult, it is better than being evil and an impostor, deceiving and being deceived, and growing worse and worse.

Paul's twofold exhortation

Timothy is to focus on two witnesses: Paul's example of a true life and his foundation, the Scriptures. Timothy has known both for most of his life. They testify to Timothy that this is the way to continue and persevere in Jesus. As Timothy continues following Paul's example and the Scriptures, he will not be deceived, nor will he deceive others.

Bad living comes from abandoning the Scriptures, the source of truth.

All Scripture is important

Paul emphasizes to Timothy the importance of continuing in the Scriptures. The apostles who wrote the gospels, the epistles, and the Revelation knew they were writing Scripture. All Scripture means the 66 books we have in the Bible that we call the Old Testament and the New Testament. All of the books in the Bible are important because they speak of Jesus. The angel in Revelation 19:10 says, "The testimony of Jesus

is the spirit of prophecy." Ultimately the whole Bible is about
what God is doing through Jesus. The Old Testament contains
the preparation for God's salvation. The New Testament is
the fulfilment of God's promises. If we only focus on the New
Testament, we ignore the foundation for those books. We
won't get the full message of God.

The Old Testament and the New Testament together are
called "canon", meaning "measuring rod." They are the writings
recognized by the church as being from God and therefore
authoritative. The church did not make them authoritative.
They only recognized them to be what they already were:
Scripture, the Word of God.

Do not add to or take away from Scripture

> For I testify to everyone who hears the words of the
> prophecy of this book: If anyone adds to these things,
> God will add to him the plagues that are written in this
> book; and if anyone takes away from the words of the
> book of this prophecy, God shall take away his part from
> the Book of Life, from the holy city, and from the things
> which are written in this book. Revelation 22:18–19
> Every word of God is pure; He is a shield to those who
> put their trust in Him. Do not add to His words, lest
> He rebuke you, and you be found a liar. Proverbs 30:5–6

Some people do add to the Scriptures. Whenever that hap-
pens, those other writings become more important than the
Bible. They become the effective authority instead of the
Bible. Groups who do this include Mormons, Seventh-Day
Adventists, Jehovah's Witnesses, and Muslims.

Others in history have taken away from the Scriptures.
Some have cut up the Scripture, saying some parts are not
the Word of God, and the ones they allow are. In this case,
people have become the authority, not the Word of God.

Another way to take away from the Scriptures is to ignore parts of the Bible and not teach them. One book often ignored is the Book of Revelation. The main emphasis is Jesus as Lord of the church and the Coming King and Judge. There might be a lot of symbols difficult to understand in the book, but Jesus is clearly shown as the Lord. The church needs that message to stand firm. What if we don't know how God is working out all things? We will see evil seem to triumph and be fearful and discouraged.

We do not add or take away from the Scriptures. We uphold them as the authority. When we teach them we have authority that comes not from men, but from God. We can also say, "Thus says the Lord."

All Scripture is given by inspiration of God

The value of the Scriptures is that they come from God. People did not think up the Scriptures. The Spirit of God came upon each writer and led him to write what the Spirit wanted to say. Over and over the message is, "Thus says the Lord." Notice in the New Testament Paul says, "Grace and peace to you from God the Father, and the Lord Jesus Christ." That is his way of saying, "Thus says the Lord."

Not only are the Scriptures His Word, but they are alive and powerful. Jesus said, "The words I speak to you are spirit and they are life."

We are not just dealing with a book. We are dealing with the Holy Spirit.

All Scripture is profitable

Just consider this first thought: God's Word is profitable. When you plant a seed in the ground, it grows and produces more fruit. It takes work to make it happen, but what is produced no man can make himself. Fruit comes from God.

What the Word produces requires work on the part of the teacher, but the effects come from God, and no one but God can do these things.

1. Profitable for doctrine. Doctrine means teaching. In the Bible we have the most important teaching of all: about God and man, how everything came to be, the purpose of everything, and the final destiny of everything. We have teaching about life, death, judgment, sin, forgiveness, salvation.

This teaching is important because it is all true. Everything written by men is fallible. They don't know everything, they don't know the future, and they are not perfect. When they don't know, they make it up.

God is perfect and knows everything from the beginning. In the Bible there are no lies, no fairy tales, nothing made up by man. It all comes from God. It is eternal. It doesn't have to change with new generations. It doesn't have to be improved. New discoveries will not make the Bible old-fashioned. It has no errors that have to be corrected.

So we can teach the Word of God, knowing that it is true, and it will reveal what people need to live right and please God.

2. Profitable for reproof. When you are reproved, you are being shown your faults. You are being told you are wrong. It's not fun to be reproved if you are innocent. But what if you are wrong? Then it is a good thing to hear that you are wrong.

When we really are wrong we need to hear it. As long as I think I am right I won't look for salvation because I don't think I need it. But if I become convinced that I truly am sinful and under the condemnation of God, then salvation is not irrelevant to me. It makes sense.

The Word of God is able to make me understand I am wrong before God. It has the logic of God, and it has the power of the Holy Spirit to convince and convict of sin, that a person is wrong before God, under His condemnation, and deserving of eternal judgment. It has power to humble a man and convert him before God. "The law of the LORD is perfect, converting the soul" (Psalm 19:7).

Then it keeps him converted by showing him where he is wrong and where he needs to repent. How much like Jesus am I right now? I need to know where I need to change. The Word of God will show me.

In 2 Samuel 11 David committed adultery, murder, and covered it up, acting like everything was all right. In His faithfulness, God reproved David by His Word through Nathan the prophet. David needed to hear that he was wrong and that things weren't okay. It was humiliating for him to be shown his wickedness, but it was better for him to be humbled than to go on in sin, headed for judgment.

3. Profitable for correction. Knowing I am wrong is good, but it's only a start. I also need to know how to get right with God. If I never learn how to get right with God, I stay a sinner, knowing I am rightfully condemned. There is no hope for me.

In the original language the word that is translated correction was used to describe setting a broken bone. If a broken bone is not set right it won't heal right. The Word of God is able to set me right so I will heal right in my life and in my faith.

4. Profitable for training in righteousness. Training in righteousness means discipline, which is the use of punishment to correct character. It's not simply punishment as an end in itself. It is the use of punishment to encourage right behaviour.

Righteousness doesn't come naturally to us. We need to be trained in it, and the Word of God will do that for us.

Solomon was taught by his father: "For the commandment is a lamp, and the teaching is a light, and reproofs for discipline are the way of life" (Proverbs 6: 23).

Hebrews 12:5–11 teaches our need for discipline from our Father:

> And you have forgotten the exhortation which speaks to you as to sons: "My son, do not despise the chastening of the LORD, nor be discouraged when you are rebuked by Him; for whom the LORD loves He chastens, and scourges every son whom He receives." If you endure chastening, God deals with you as with sons; for what son is there whom a father does not chasten? But if you are without chastening, of which all have become partakers, then you are illegitimate and not sons. Furthermore, we have had human fathers who corrected us, and we paid them respect. Shall we not much more readily be in subjection to the Father of spirits and live? For they indeed for a few days chastened us as seemed best to them, but He for our profit, that we may be partakers of His holiness. Now no chastening seems to be joyful for the present, but painful; nevertheless, afterward it yields the peaceable fruit of righteousness to those who have been trained by it.

We are not truly sons of God if we refuse His discipline. Training in righteousness of the Scriptures is absolutely profitable.

5. That the man of God may be complete. Complete means specially adapted, having everything needed to be effective and to fulfil the purpose and calling of God. His Word

HANDLING ACCURATELY THE WORD OF TRUTH

is a complete school and teacher to prepare you. It will also prepare your listeners as you teach His Word.

Sometimes I am tempted to think that I need more money to minister successfully, or more machines or miracles. Paul says what we need is to have our characters trained by the Word of God in order to accurately and powerfully deliver that word to others.

Application

Paul applies his teaching to Timothy, exhorting him to preach the Word, to be ready in season and out of season, to convince and rebuke, and exhort with all patience and teaching. He solemnly charges Timothy by God to preach the Word.

Do you sense Paul's urgency? He wrote this at the beginning of the Christian era. Nearly two thousand years later, we are in the days he spoke about. Men in the church act like those outside the church. People do not endure sound teaching, but heap up teachers who tell them what they want to hear. They are turning aside to fables. They are lovers of pleasure, not lovers of God.

We might sigh and be discouraged, but that would be unbelief. Instead, let's take heart. This confirms the Word of God. He said it would happen, and it has. It should make us even more confident in what the rest of the Bible says. All of God's Word will be fulfilled.

Paul's command still holds for us today. We need to preach and teach all the Word of God to let it work in us and in our people. Isaiah 55:10–11 is still true:

"For as the rain comes down, and the snow from heaven, and do not return there, but water the earth, and make it bring forth and bud, that it may give seed to the sower and bread to the eater, so shall My word be that goes forth from My mouth; it shall not return to Me void, but it shall accomplish what I please, and it shall prosper in the thing for which I sent it."

We know we are fulfilling the will of God as we raise up men and women who know His Word and are equipped to do the work of ministry. Our reward will be to hear Him say on that Day, "Well done, good and faithful servant. Enter into the joy of your Master."

3. Observe one verse

We want to teach what the Bible says and let it speak for itself. This happens as we teach through the Bible, book by book, chapter by chapter, verse by verse.

In order to do that, we need to know how to accurately find out what the Bible is saying. We study the text of the Bible. To study is to look closely and carefully at something in order to learn about it. Studying the Bible is a process of asking questions and looking to the text to find answers.

Paul urges Timothy to study the Scriptures:

Be diligent to present yourself approved to God as a workman who does not need to be ashamed, handling accurately the word of truth. 2 Timothy 2:15

Our first session studying the Bible will be to look at one verse and see how many questions we can ask about it. From there we can go on to look at a paragraph, and then a whole chapter.

All Scripture is good. So I picked this verse:

The fear of the LORD is the beginning of knowledge, but fools despise wisdom and instruction. Proverbs 1:7

Define, ask questions, answer, write

We begin to study by looking at the words used. Do you know what they mean? We assume we know what a word means, but if we try to define it, we find our definitions are fuzzy.

This shows we don't really grasp the concept. So the rule is: if you can't define a word quickly and easily, look it up in a dictionary. You will be surprised how much you can learn that way! I often look up words I think I'm familiar with in order to learn from the clarity of the dictionary.

We ask questions that the text can answer. We'll see later on this chapter what kind of questions to ask.

Write down what you learn: the definitions, the answers, even the questions. Use lots of paper. As you write you will think more about it. You might discover some new relationship of ideas that you have never considered before. I have found that when I write out my observations I develop my thoughts and discover insights to the Scripture that I have been trying to understand.

Writing out your thoughts keeps them in front of you so you can look at them. I don't like to juggle too many thoughts in my head. I like to see them and evaluate them objectively.

What kind of text are we looking at?

The Bible is composed of 66 writings. It's a history book. It's a book of poems. It's a biography. It's a how-to manual. It is composed of different genres of writing.

One genre is **exposition**, writing that explains something. The writer has an idea or ideas he wants to communicate. He develops his concepts point by point. Then he shows the practical implications of these ideas. The New Testament epistles are examples of exposition.

There are genres of **history** and **narrative**, that is, accounts of what has happened in the past, telling of people who participated, of the results of what happened, the lessons learned, and so on. **Biography** is a genre of history that looks at a person's life. The **Gospels** are the history surrounding the life of Jesus.

Parables are stories that make a point, a conclusion, or a lesson. Most are found in the Gospels, but they are also scattered through the Bible.

Proverbs and **wisdom literature** are concerned with living rightly in harmony with the law of God.

Prophecy looks at the future and applies that to living rightly in the present. The Book of Revelation is prophecy of a kind called **apocalyptic**, because it speaks of the last days and uses many symbols to communicate its message. The Book of Daniel has parts considered to be apocalyptic.

We make ourselves aware of these different kinds of writing in the Bible so that we can understand what each kind of writing says in its own way. The truths communicated by a proverb are different from those communicated by history. We interpret according to what is being communicated and how it is being said.

Therefore we notice that Proverbs 1:7 is from the genre of **proverbs** and **wisdom literature.**

We should also be aware that much of the Book of Proverbs is written in Hebrew poetry. Hebrew poetry rhymes ideas instead of sounds, as we think of English poetry. This is called **parallelism,** and there are several ways to do it. One is where the first line makes a statement and the next line agrees with that statement using different words. For example:

O LORD, do not rebuke me in Your anger,
Nor chasten me in Your hot displeasure. Psalm 6:1

Here are two different ways to say the same thing. Because they are similar we can use one line to interpret the other. Anger is compared to hot displeasure. Rebuke and chasten are compared.

Another kind of parallelism is where the second line is a contrast to the first, like this:
Before I was afflicted I went astray,
but now I keep Your word. Psalm 119:67
There is a "before" and an "after" to this statement. We can ask, "What is the difference between "before" and "after", and what made the difference?"

We notice Proverbs 1:7 is two lines. Do the lines agree with one another, or do they contrast each other? (Answer: the first line contrasts with the second.) We'll see how we can use the contrasts as we continue our study. Let's start asking questions of our Scripture.

The fear of the LORD is the beginning of knowledge, but fools despise wisdom and instruction. Proverbs 1:7

What is knowledge? I looked in a Hebrew dictionary: it means knowledge that comes from observing and thinking, and knowledge that comes from experience.

So because the lines contrast, could you say that fools aren't observing or thinking, or aren't experiencing God? (Answer: yes)

What is the fear of the Lord? The dictionary says: profound reverence and awe, godliness and holy fear.

Reverence is profound respect mingled with love and awe.

Since we decided these two lines were contrasts, could we say that fools don't reverence God, don't respect God, don't love God? (Answer: yes)

What does beginning mean? The dictionary says: the point in time or space at which something starts. There's nothing before the beginning.

So fools haven't started at knowledge yet? (Answer: yes)

What does despise mean? It means: feel contempt or a deep repugnance for. Do I know what contempt or repugnance is? If I don't understand the definition, it doesn't help much. We can work around that by looking up words till we start to get the idea. I keep searching for meaning like this:

What does contempt mean? The feeling that a person or a thing is beneath consideration, worthless, or deserving scorn.

What does repugnance mean? Intense disgust.

What does disgust mean? A feeling of revulsion or profound disapproval aroused by something unpleasant or offensive.

What does disapproval mean? Possession or expression of an unfavourable opinion.

What does unfavourable mean? Expressing or showing a lack of approval or support.

Is a person right when he thinks that God is wrong?

What is the attitude when someone thinks they are smarter than God? Pride, I think.

So someone who despises wisdom and instruction also hates them, and thinks they are unpleasant and disagreeable.

It leads me to ask: Why would I think that? Maybe because I don't want to be told I'm wrong, especially by God, because I want to do what I want, and I don't want anyone telling me what to do. That is pride again, it seems to me.

What does wisdom mean? The dictionary says: the quality of having experience, knowledge, and good judgement; the quality of being wise.

What does instruction mean? I looked in a Hebrew dictionary. It means discipline, chastening, correction.

What does discipline mean? The dictionary says: the practice of training people to obey rules or a code of behaviour, using punishment to correct disobedience.

What does chastening mean? (this is a quote from my dictionary: 1a: to subject to pain, suffering, deprivation, or misfortune in order to correct, strengthen, or perfect in character, in mental or spiritual qualities, or in conduct: discipline [whom the Lord loveth he chasteneth Hebrews 12:6 Authorized Version])

This is a hint from the dictionary to look at Hebrews 12, and when we do that, we find a lot there that explains discipline. Look for the answers to these questions:

Who does discipline?

Who is discipline for?

Does this discipline feel good at the time?

What does discipline produce later?

What if we don't receive discipline?

These are all good questions for Hebrews 12 that can add to our understanding of Proverbs 1:7. But now let's get back to our text.

What is a fool? Proverbs 1:7 says a fool is one who despises wisdom and knowledge. Because of the contrasting lines in the poetry, we can see that a fool also despises the fear of the Lord.

In the Proverbs and wisdom literature, a fool is not stupid mentally, but stupid morally. He might be a smart person otherwise, but if he doesn't fear God, he is really foolish.

That makes me ask more questions:

Why is it foolish to not fear God? As I think about what the Bible says, it seems it's because God will judge every person. Everyone will end up in heaven or hell depending on how God judges them.

Who will go to heaven? All those who receive Jesus as their Lord and their Saviour and live to honour Him.

Who will go to hell? All those who reject Jesus and live any way they want because they don't believe in Jesus or God or judgement.

What does a fool want? We know what a fool doesn't want: instruction (we learned that means discipline).

What is the opposite of discipline? The dictionary knows: dissoluteness, which means indulging in sensuous pleasures.

Indulgence, an inability to resist the gratification of whims and desires, unrestraint, the quality of lacking restraint.

What is restraint? Self-control.

What is self-control? The ability to control oneself, in particular one's emotions and desires or the expression of them in one's behaviour, especially in difficult situations.

What is important about self-control? The opposite is no control over self. Or rather, something else than you has the control. That could be pleasure, drugs, alcohol, gambling, sex, eating, or something other than God. Can that be good? What happens if the Lord is your shepherd? What if something else besides God is your shepherd? Because I read the Bible constantly, this reminds me of Psalm 49:14 where it actually says of the wicked, "Death shall be their shepherd."

So it seems that a fool doesn't want God ruling over him, but because he has no self-control, he will have something that is not God ruling over him, ultimately, death. Is that a good idea?

Write the verse in your own words

This is an exercise in making the meaning of the text clear. When you can express what the verse means in different words, then you have grasped the idea. You are now able to give the idea to others so they will understand it as well.

This is not easy. It is easier to just rewrite the verse, rearranging the same words. What I try to do is write a sentence getting all of the ideas in as best as I can. Usually the sentence is too long and is grammatically awful. But it gives me something to look at and ask myself what is wrong with it, what is right, and what needs to change. I keep writing the sentence, throwing out what is not necessary or not right, until I feel that my sentence says what the verse is about. It's a lot of work, but when I am done, I know what the verse is all about.

Let's try that here.

> To start knowing like God says I ought to know includes awesome respect for God and training in righteousness. If I don't like that, it makes me a fool.

My first try has two sentences but I want to get it all in one. Did I get everything? I'm not satisfied with this. I'll try it again.

> Fearing God and accepting His discipline for me will start me on the path of knowing the truth, but if I don't humble myself and let Him tell me when I'm wrong, I'll never learn anything worth knowing.

Hmmm ... That's kind of a long sentence. Did I get everything in that I have observed? Does it make sense? Is it true, according to the proverb?

I like that. Can you write a better sentence?

4. Observe a paragraph

Now that we have worked to study one verse, we want to do the same thing to a paragraph of verses. The difference is that we have a larger number of verses. The similarity is that the verses together have a meaning, and that's what we want to find. We begin by observing the details of each verse. Then we determine what the verses together say: the point of the account. Then we write in one sentence what is happening.

What paragraph of Scripture?

There is no special reason that I pick the Gospel of Matthew, chapter 11:1–6. It could be any paragraph of Scripture because all Scripture is profitable. I trust this will speak to us as we ask questions and we listen for answers.

1 Now it came to pass, when Jesus finished commanding His twelve disciples, that He departed from there to teach and to preach in their cities.

2 And when John had heard in prison about the works of Christ, he sent two of his disciples

3 and said to Him, "Are You the Coming One, or do we look for another?"

4 Jesus answered and said to them, "Go and tell John the things which you hear and see:

5 "The blind see and the lame walk; the lepers are cleansed and the deaf hear; the dead are raised up and the poor have the gospel preached to them.

6 "And blessed is he who is not offended because of Me."

Verse 1 ♦ Where is Jesus? He is on a teaching tour in the cities around Galilee. It's a guess because it doesn't say exactly. But it says He was teaching in their cities. If it was the disciples' cities, it was the area around Galilee because that's where most of the disciples came from.

What has He been doing? He was commanding His disciples and teaching them to send them out to preach the kingdom and to heal. We learn this from "Jesus finished commanding His disciples." When we look at what happened before this, we see that almost all of chapter 10 is about Jesus preparing the disciples for this mission.

What does Jesus do after He sends them out? Jesus Himself leaves the place and goes on His own tour of cities, teaching, preaching, and healing. Even though He has just sent out the disciples, He doesn't stop doing the same work. He could stop and say, "I'm the leader, now these guys will do all the work and I can relax." But He keeps going.

Why does He do that? This is not answered directly in the text so we have to make a careful guess. We notice He continues to practice what He has taught His disciples. We remember that Jesus said He came to seek and save the lost. So we can answer that He does this because He wants to, not because He has to, as a demonstration for His disciples. That's a guess. We can test it by asking, "Does that conclusion agree with what we know about Jesus?"

Verse 2 ♦ Which John is it? The text doesn't immediately say. It's not the apostle John because Jesus just sent him out to preach and teach. Later on we read that Jesus talks to the crowds about someone named John, and it's obvious that He is talking about John the Baptist.

Where is John? The text says he's in prison.

Why is he there? The text doesn't say. So we have to ask if there are any other places in the Gospels that could give us the information. Here's where reading the Bible regularly comes in handy (which we will talk about in chapter 8): we remember that in Luke 3:19–20 John rebuked Herod the tetrarch for marrying his brother's wife. It was not lawful, according to the law of God. Herod arrested John and put him in prison.

How did John hear these things? His disciples told him, so they must have tried to visit John and had been allowed to see him in prison. Could it have been risky for them to visit John?

What did John hear about? It says they told John about the works of Christ. We might ask then, what does Christ mean? What works did Jesus do? He taught and preached and did miracles of healing and casting out demons.

What did John do after that? It says he sent two of his disciples to ask Jesus a question.

Verse 3 ♦ What does "the Coming One" mean? It's a title for the Messiah (in Hebrew) or the Christ (in Greek). So John is asking if Jesus is the Christ. But that's not the full question. He is asking if Jesus is the Messiah, or should he and his disciples wait for another person, who would be the Messiah.

Why would John ask that? This forces us to guess because it doesn't say in the text. But if we imagine ourselves in John's position, we can ask some questions and get some good answers.

Does John like being in prison? Probably not. I wouldn't like being there.

Is Jesus powerful? Yes, He is. He is raising people from the dead and healing blind people.

If I were John and hearing about these things, I would ask, "Why doesn't Jesus get me out of here?" I might even ask, "Did He forget about me, that I'm His faithful forerunner? I did my job—I pointed Him out so people might believe in Him. The Messiah wouldn't leave me in prison. Why am I still in prison? Maybe Jesus isn't the Messiah."

Even though John saw the Holy Spirit descend on Jesus and abide on Him, he is questioning who Jesus is.

Does it sound like John believes in Jesus? It sounds to me like John is either doubting Jesus, or reminding Him, "Hey, don't forget about me!" John might be disappointed in Jesus. At the very least, he is questioning Jesus and is not sure about Him.

What was John's mission? John the Baptist is the one sent by God to preach repentance in the wilderness and ultimately point out the Messiah when He comes. Regular Bible reading (Chapter 8 again!) helps us remember that he was prophesied in Malachi 4 and Isaiah 40 as the one to come before the Messiah.

Was he successful in his mission? Yes. We read about it in Matthew 3, Luke 3, and John 1. He pointed to Jesus and said, "Behold! The Lamb of God who takes away the sin of the world!" (John 1:29).

He also said in the same chapter, "I did not know Him; but that He should be revealed to Israel, therefore I came baptizing with water." And John bore witness, saying, "I saw the Spirit descending from heaven like a dove, and He remained upon Him. I did not know Him, but He who sent me to baptize with water said to me, 'Upon whom you see the Spirit descending, and remaining on Him, this is He who baptizes with the Holy Spirit.' And I have seen and testified that this is the Son of God" (John 1:31–34).

So John was sent by God for a mission, and he completed that mission.

What happened after that? John's ministry became smaller and smaller (we read that in John 3:26), then he was arrested and put in prison.

Verses 4–5 ✦ How does Jesus answer John's question? Jesus doesn't answer either yes or no. It's not a direct answer, like, "I am the Coming One."

What does Jesus tell John's disciples to do? He tells them to go and tell John the things which they hear and see.

What are people called who tell what they hear and see? They are called "witnesses."

What do the disciples hear and see? They saw the things Jesus talked about: the blind see, the lame walk, lepers are cleansed, the deaf hear, the dead are raised up. They also hear Jesus preaching the Gospel to them.

What would that be like? Probably like the Sermon on the Mount.

What effect did that sermon have? At the end of the Sermon on the Mount, it says that the people were astonished at His teaching for He taught them as one having authority, and not as the scribes (Matthew 7:28–29). They had never heard anyone like Jesus.

What is important about these miracles? We look around in the Bible and find that these miracles are prophesied in Isaiah 35 and 61. The Messiah will do these things.

What are the miracles for? They prove who Jesus is: the Messiah, the Coming One, the One who fulfils prophecy.

Verse 6 ✦ What does "blessed" mean? Blessed means "happy" with this added benefit: made happy by God.

What does "offended" mean? It means displeased, hurt, annoyed, angry, irritated, resentful.

What does it mean to be offended at somebody? It means that you don't like what they are doing to you. You say what they are doing is bad.

What does it mean to be offended at Christ? Is that a good thing or a bad thing? It means that you don't like whatever Christ is doing to you. You think it is a bad thing.

Why would John be offended at Christ? Another guess: because Jesus isn't doing what John wants: to get him out of prison.

Who is right, John or Jesus? That's an amazing question but we have to ask it. Is John right to be offended, or is Jesus right to leave John in prison?

How can John (and we) decide this? Jesus has given him the tools to work it out. He can listen to what the two disciples say about Jesus. He must decide, first of all, who is Jesus? Does He fulfil the Scriptures? Is He God?

Then secondly, for John to be blessed, he has to not be offended at Jesus. Why is John is prison? The truth is that God could get him out immediately, but He hasn't. He has left him there. It must be the will of God for John to be in prison.

Can John trust God and be at peace in prison? He can if he can trust God without having any answers. Jesus doesn't give John any answers. John just has to trust in God that He knows what He is doing.

Write a sentence to describe what is happening in the paragraph in your own words.

This is my first attempt:

> Jesus sends the disciples off to teach and preach and does the same Himself, and John's disciples come and tell him about what Jesus is doing, so he tells his disciples to ask Jesus if He's the Messiah, and Jesus tells them to tell John

what they have heard and seen, and to tell him that he is blessed if he is not offended by Him.

Now that is a terrible sentence, because it says the same thing as the verses themselves. I will try it again, using different words, to write a decent, short sentence.

While Jesus and the disciples teach and preach, John the Baptist sends to ask Him if He is the Messiah, and Jesus sends back the disciples as witnesses to who He is, and admonishes John that He is doing right to leave John there in prison.

That is more of what we have learned as a result of our asking questions, but it is still a bad sentence. I forgot to add John's disciples and suddenly they show up in the second part. How can I fix this sentence? I'll try it again.

John, in prison, wonders why Jesus doesn't get him out of prison and sends two disciples to ask Him if He is really the Messiah, to which Jesus sends the disciples back to witness what they have seen and heard, and to gently say John is wrong to not trust Him as the Messiah.

It's still too long of a sentence, but I'm getting smoother, and I'm starting to get to the point of the verses. But I'm not there yet. I did get rid of the part of Jesus teaching and preaching, because that doesn't seem to be the main point of the passage. So now I'm asking, what is the main point of the passage? Try it again.

John wonders why Jesus leaves him in prison, and Jesus tells him to decide who He is, and then trust in Him, that He does what is right always.

It's shorter, but still not there.

John doesn't like it in prison and wonders why Jesus doesn't get him out, questioning who He is, and Jesus replies with testimony about who He is, and gently encourages John to trust Him without getting answers. Now, I like that better. Does that explain what is going on in these verses? Can you write a better sentence?

5. Interpreting the Scriptures

Paul encouraged Timothy, "Be diligent to present yourself approved to God as a workman who does not need to be ashamed, handling accurately the word of truth" (2 Timothy 2:15). In order to handle the Word accurately, we need to interpret it. That means to explain the meaning of the Scriptures. We need to be able to say, "**This** is what it says," and also be able to say, "This is what is **doesn't** say."

To get the right interpretation is important for the following reasons.

We want to say what God says
God takes His Word seriously. We are not to add to it, nor are we to take away from it, or change it in any way. If we get the interpretation wrong, we are doing just that.

God spoke through Jeremiah about those who called themselves prophets, claiming to speak His Word, but they were making up their own message.

> Thus says the LORD of hosts: "Do not listen to the words of the prophets who prophesy to you. They make you worthless; they speak a vision of their own heart, not from the mouth of the LORD. They continually say to those who despise Me, 'The LORD has said, "You shall have peace"'; and to everyone who walks according to the dictates of his own heart, they say, 'No evil shall come upon you.'"

For who has stood in the counsel of the Lord, and has perceived and heard His word? Who has marked His word and heard it?

Behold, a whirlwind of the Lord has gone forth in fury—a violent whirlwind! It will fall violently on the head of the wicked. The anger of the Lord will not turn back until He has executed and performed the thoughts of His heart. In the latter days you will understand it perfectly.

"I have not sent these prophets, yet they ran. I have not spoken to them, yet they prophesied. But if they had stood in My counsel, and had caused My people to hear My words, then they would have turned them from their evil way and from the evil of their doings.

"Am I a God near at hand," says the Lord, "And not a God afar off? Can anyone hide himself in secret places, so I shall not see him?" says the Lord; "Do I not fill heaven and earth?" says the Lord. I have heard what the prophets have said who prophesy lies in My name, saying, 'I have dreamed, I have dreamed!' How long will this be in the heart of the prophets who prophesy lies? Indeed they are prophets of the deceit of their own heart, who try to make My people forget My name by their dreams which everyone tells his neighbor, as their fathers forgot My name for Baal.

"The prophet who has a dream, let him tell a dream; and he who has My word, let him speak My word faithfully. What is the chaff to the wheat?" says the Lord. Is not My word like a fire?" says the Lord, "And like a hammer that breaks the rock in pieces?

"Therefore behold, I am against the prophets," says the Lord, "who steal My words every one from his neighbor.

> Behold, I am against the prophets," says the Lord, "who
> use their tongues and say, 'He says.' Behold, I am against
> those who prophesy false dreams," says the Lord, "and
> tell them, and cause My people to err by their lies and by
> their recklessness. Yet I did not send them or command
> them; therefore they shall not profit this people at all,"
> says the Lord. Jeremiah 23:16–32

That big block of Scripture warns that prophets are only
to speak the word they receive from God. When we correctly interpret the Scriptures we can say, "Thus says the Lord,"
and it really is what He is saying.

In order to live right, we must believe right

How important is truth to our lives? When we believe what
is true, then we will live rightly. We won't be deceived; we
won't be cheated. But what if we believe something that is
false, and live our lives according to our false understanding?
Then our lives will not show the reality of God. We won't be
true witnesses of God.

Some people say it doesn't matter what you believe as long
as you are sincere. Sincere people in non-Christian religions
and cults believe something false about Jesus, usually that He
is not the Son of God, or that He is not God. The apostle
John says if they don't believe rightly about Jesus, they don't
have God.

> Who is the liar but the one who denies that Jesus is the
> Christ? This is the antichrist, the one who denies the
> Father and the Son. Whoever denies the Son does not
> have the Father; the one who confesses the Son has the
> Father also. 1 John 2:22–23

Those who deny that Jesus is God do not have the Father.
They might hold to God as they understand Him, yet in real-

ity, they are greatly deceived and cheated. They do not have the true God. They believe they are right with God when in reality they oppose Him. A classic example of this is Saul of Tarsus who believed he was serving God as he persecuted believers in Jesus. Therefore it is not enough to be sincere, we have to have truth. In order to live rightly we must accurately understand the Scripture.

Correct interpretation leads to right application

This is closely related to the last point. What if we get the meaning of a Scripture wrong? Then we also get the applications wrong as well. We end up doing something God didn't say to do.

A leader of a movement of churches read in Deuteronomy 16:16 that "They shall appear before the Lord empty-handed." He thought that was striking and unusual. He thought to himself, "Why appear before God empty-handed?" He decided that it meant that they weren't to have their own agenda before God, but seek Him and say, "Lord, here we are, empty-handed, please fill our hands with Your purpose." He taught this to his pastors at their conferences, and for years they did this when they gathered together.

It wasn't until years later that the leader found he had read the verse wrong. It says "They shall **not** appear before the Lord empty-handed (*emphasis mine*)." His observation was wrong, so that his interpretation was wrong, and so was his application of the verse. It is a good idea to seek the Lord for His purposes, but this verse does not teach that.

We want to understand what God is saying so that we can apply the teaching correctly.

It is easier to interpret after much observation

Much thorough observation will help us get the right interpretation. The more we observe and ask questions and get answers, the easier it will be to say, "This is what the text is saying." The less time we spend observing, the more we have to guess. There is more risk because we really don't know what the text is saying.

When we have a lot of observations, they will lead us to the right interpretation because they will rule out any other. The right interpretation has to take into account all that we have seen in the text. If our interpretation contradicts an observation, it can't be the right interpretation. The right meaning of a text should fit just like Cinderella's glass slipper. This is a fairy tale, I know, but it has a good point.

For those of you who don't know the story, there was a prince trying to find a beautiful girl who ran away from him, leaving behind a single glass slipper. The prince didn't know her name or where to find her. He decided that he would look throughout his kingdom for the girl who fit the glass slipper. Many women pushed and shoved and twisted to make the slipper fit, but their feet were either too big or too small. Only the one who fit the slipper would be the right girl. And he eventually found her, and they lived happily ever after.

The point is: the correct interpretation will fit naturally. We are not trying to find just any meaning or force the Scripture to fit our theory. We are trying to find the true meaning. It should be just like in the story: the right girl put the glass slipper on, and the fit was perfect. We shouldn't have to push and shove and twist Scripture to make our interpretation fit. It should fit exactly. It should account for all of our observations. It should fit within the context of the rest of Scripture. If the interpretation clashes with another Scripture, it can't be right. We need to go back and observe more, so we have more to guide us to the right meaning.

So this is an important rule: **The more time we spend in observation, the less time we have to spend in interpretation.**

Interpretation Hazards to Avoid

Misreading the text. "For the love of money is a root of all sorts of evil", or "Money is the root of all evil"? Ignorance of what the text says is the unpardonable sin of interpretation. It shows that you really haven't done your homework. You've skipped the first step in Bible study method—observation.

Distorting the text. Distort: To twist out of the true meaning or proportion. Making the text say what you want it to say, not what it actually says.

Contradicting the text. That is, an interpretation contrary to what God has actually said, like the serpent did in Genesis 3:1–4, or something that contradicts God's character.

Subjectivism. The meaning of the text is in the text, not what I *feel* the text means. The text means what the writer meant it to mean: one thing, not several things at the same time. There might be many ways to apply that one thing, but the text means only one thing.

Relativism. The meaning of the text does not change with the passing of time or changes in culture, technology, or social morals. What it meant when written is what it means today.

Overconfidence. Pride makes one arrogant and unteachable. "No one can understand the Scriptures who has not walked with them for one hundred years. This is true. We are all beggars." (Note found in Martin Luther's pocket after his death.) As our knowledge grows, so should our humility. Do we know everything? A teacher needs to be teachable.

Identify what kind of text you are studying

Exposition. Straightforward factual communication. Epistles generally consist of doctrine then application. The reasoning progresses to a conclusion. There is a "red thread" of continuity.

Narrative and biography. Accounts of events, incidents, and people's lives. Look for plot (what happens), characterization (what happens to the people in the account? How do they change / not change?), what is true to life (what questions does the text raise? How do the people deal with problems? What lessons do they learn?).

Parables. Parable is brief story that illustrates moral principle. Look for the point, similar to the point of a joke.

Poetry. Look for parallelism of Hebrew poetry: rhyming thought, not words. Sometimes it repeats a thought, sometimes it extends a thought. It can also can contrast ideas (*see discussion on p. 35*). Wisdom is the art of living rightly and beautifully, concerned with actions and their consequences. It is hard to live rightly. It is easy to live badly.

Prophecy and Apocalyptic. This is mainly Daniel and the Book of Revelation. Two aspects of the message: a warning to the situation of that day when it was written, and a description of the situation of the future. Look for partial as well as ultimate fulfilments. Symbols in Revelation are often first used elsewhere in Scripture, which helps to interpret them. Avoid being overly dogmatic about minute interpretation of detail. Look for the big picture of action.

What will keep your interpretation accurate?

Content. Knowing what the text says keeps you from distorting the text. Don't abstract too much away from the text.

Context. Context is the parts of something written or spoken that immediately precede and follow a word or passage and clarify its meaning. Look at a Scripture in the bigger picture of the chapter to see its meaning.

Literary, what happens before and after a text

Historical, what period the text occurs.

Geographical, where does it take place? What kind of terrain? How far? How deep? How high?

Theological, how much did the people know about God at the time?

Comparison. Use reference books to get facts: Bible dictionaries, atlases, handbooks.

Use a concordance to check usages of words, contexts, where people are mentioned in Scripture.

Commentaries. See if the writers agree with your interpretation. Get information from men who have sifted through all the literature and summarize different viewpoints. Get insight into language, culture, variant readings of text, etc. Use these last rather than first. We want to first observe the text for ourselves, then see what everyone else has said.

(This material adapted from *Living by the Book*, by Howard Hendricks and William Hendricks, Moody Press, Chicago, 2007. In my opinion it's the best book ever on how to study the Bible. I recommend that you get this book and learn from a master!)

6. Now what? How to make application

We have worked hard to **observe** the text of Scripture. We have worked hard to **interpret,** so we can say, "This is what the text is saying." Now that we have found the meaning of the text we want to take it a step further and make it practical. We ask the question, "So what if this is true? What am I supposed to do in the light of this?"

Sometimes the implications of our message will not be clear. People will not know how to respond. This happened to Peter in Acts 2:37:

> Now when they heard this, they were cut to the heart, and said to Peter and the rest of the apostles, "Men and brethren, what shall we do?"

It wasn't because Peter was a bad teacher; on the contrary, he did a great job. But now the people needed to know what to do. Peter told them the **application** to his message, the answer to the question, "Since this is true, what do I do now?" That's what we want to learn to do.

Find the principles and commands of the text and apply them

The purpose of study is to put the teaching into action. If all we do is hear the message but do not do what it says, we are deceiving ourselves. We want to encourage our listeners to respond to God.

Ask questions, put the application in the form of a question. What will happen if we do what the Scriptures say? What will happen if we don't?

Ask what God would have you do in response to that passage.

Is there an **example** for me to follow?

Is there a **sin** to avoid?

Is there a **promise** to claim?

Is there a **prayer** to repeat?

Is there a **command** to obey?

Is there a **condition** to meet?

Is there a **verse** to memorize?

Is there an **error** to mark?

Is there a **challenge** to face?

Put yourself into the passage and apply it to yourself. What applies to you will often apply to others.

7. Turn study results into a message

So far, we have been doing word studies and observations, leading to interpreting the text. We do it to understand the main idea, and understand the relation of sub points to the main idea. Outlining is a tool for analysis. The message is already there in the text. We want to grasp the structure of the text. Our outline becomes the starting point for the message.

Make an outline for the section

A. Rough the thoughts out on paper, find the natural breaks in the text.

B. Look for the ideas, statements, and reasons. Number the main points.

C. Decide what are the subpoints that go under each main point.

D. Consider how the ideas all relate, and only then find the main title for the section.

Determine what is to be taught—the intent

A. Ask yourself: "What does a Christian need to know from this passage? What is he to do?" List the things.

B. What principles are being taught in this passage? List the principles.

Your job is to make people learn the concepts and principles derived from the text.

Structure of a Message: Beginning, Middle, End

A. Beginning: Making an introduction

1. Show how the passage is relevant to your hearers. Why are we considering this Scripture passage and not another? Why should anyone listen to what this Scripture has to say?

2. Show context. If you are doing a series of related messages, how does this passage fit into the context? You may need to do a short review to make sure the people follow your idea, but get to the point.

3. Be brief and potent! Make the most of your first twenty-five words.

4. Create interest. Ask questions; create tension that your teaching will resolve.

5. Don't let writing an introduction slow you down. If you are short on time write this last. Then you will have a better idea of how to start.

6. You can read the section of Scripture you want to teach so that people can hear it in context before you study. Another way is to read a passage in sections, teaching one section at a time, then make application for the whole passage at the end.

B. Middle: This is what you want to teach

1. Have a plan. There should be a "red thread", a sense of logical progression so that each point adds understanding. One idea should lead to another, and not be a jumble of ideas for the listener to figure out.

2. Explain the text. Give supporting facts and insight from your preparation, so that the thrust of the text is clear. Apply certain parts of the text along the way.

C. End: Resolve the tension, give a sense of finality
1. Land the plane, don't circle the runway
By this I mean: make a real ending. I read about John Coltrane, a jazz saxophonist known for half-hour solos, complaining to Miles Davis, "I don't know how to end a solo!" Miles said, "Take your horn out of your mouth."

Definitely end the message, don't go on and on. But we shouldn't merely stop talking. We should make messages that have a definite point at their conclusion. Instead of improvising some kind of ending, we should know where we are going and then bring our listeners along with us.

Never say: "And this really will be my last point." That distracts attention away from the message onto the clock. Don't work against yourself. If you realise you are going too long, speed things up, get to the point, end the message.

2. Apply the Scripture
The message points to something to acknowledge, to trust in, to act upon. Apply that. Make it practical. Ask the question, "Are you doing that?"

3. Other ways to end:
A summary, an illustration, a quotation, a question, a prayer.

Make Your Point
There are only so many ways to make the point to your message have meaning to somebody else, to cause them to grasp the message you want them to learn.

Repeat. Say the same thing again. People listening to you don't have the opportunity to rewind you to hear a statement over again. Add emphasis by repeating a statement several times throughout the teaching.

Restate. Say the same thing but use different words. In other words, repeat the thought but vary the language. Finding a new way of expressing an idea enables you to emphasize your point without being tiresome.

Define. Definition establishes what must be included and excluded by a term or statement. Words can be abstract. Your job is to make them concrete. Use examples.

Explanation. How does a thing work? How big is it? How much? What does an idea imply? How does it relate to other ideas? Use examples.

Facts. Use observations, examples, statistics, and other data that may be verified apart from the preacher. Take ideas; make them practical in application. Make sure you verify your facts! Sixty-seven percent of all quoted statistics are false! I just made that up!

Tell a story. Restate the action. Amplify, update it, bring out the true-to-life aspects. Use a story to supply background history, setting, or personalities involved in a passage. Use experiences from your own life, but watch out for always making yourself the hero. If you tell the same stories over and over your listeners may get bored. Do not use stories about family or friends without their permission.

Illustration. An illustration is like a window that lets in light to the room. It's supposed to make your point clear. Restate, explain, prove or apply ideas by relating them to easily understood experiences or things. You can explain with examples from the Bible, from your reading, personal experience, observation of life, etc. The whole creation can be used to illustrate spiritual concepts.

Quotation. Quote someone if they say it in a way so fitting that you can't improve on it. Don't go out of your way to find quotes. Let quotes come naturally from the things you read, otherwise, it may come across as artificial.

Humour. Tell a joke, get sarcastic, or ironic, but be careful to be appropriate. Humour is easy to overdo. Don't be lightweight and trivial. Let your humour be natural.

Making Notes

Notes are to help you remember what you want to say and keep you on topic so you present a clear, understandable, and memorable message. It is a practical consideration that can help you do your best spiritual work.

Format options for making notes

Outline. This is a "less is more" format. Decide whether a point is a main point, or a sub point, or a sub-sub-point, etc. When your thought is clear, you can speak clearly. If it's all a jumble, you will lose people in the confusion. Decide what are the main points and what are the supporting points.

Outlining can help clarify, organize, and reveal structure as you write it out.

Pro: There is a greater sense of structure, it is visually easy to follow; it makes it easier to get the message out.

Con: If your outline doesn't have enough detail, it might not remind you of what you wanted to say.

Write message out in full. This means write every word out from your introduction to your ending.

Pro: It helps you to think in paragraphs. Writing helps to work out your thoughts, how you want to express things. It helps to decide on how to make transitions. From there you can depart from the manuscript when the Holy Spirit gives you inspiration at the moment to add to your message.

Con: It is a discipline to write clearly. It's difficult to skip points if you find that you are rearranging a message as you speak (which can happen). Being tied to your manuscript can inhibit your freedom.

No notes at all. Some prefer to let the Holy Spirit use their preparation and exercise their prophetic gift. This can be profitable when you get too distracted by using notes. Sometimes God uses this to make us more dependent upon Him. A disadvantage to this method is there is a risk of becoming dull to listen to if we are not quick thinkers. We might find ourselves getting confused and confuse others if we say things as we think of them. If we are organized, it makes it easier for people to follow what we say.

Experiment until you find what works best for you. Pray for insight, read books on teaching, think your method out. Then there is less to think about when you're working under a deadline.

Practical considerations for making notes

Choose appropriate size paper. Think about where you teach. Do you have a desk or podium to speak from? Or is your Bible on your lap? Make your paper size fit the environment you teach in for maximum efficiency.

Write legibly! You must be able to read your own notes! They should serve you, not make your life difficult.

Illustrations. Write out your stories and illustrations with enough detail so you will know what you wanted to say. What you remember now might be a mystery the next day or one year from now.

How many pages in your message? As many as you need! Waste forests, if you have to! Watch people; see what their capacity is. There is no use pouring more water than the cup can hold.

After you get a feel for the average length of a study, you can use the average number of pages to determine what the length of study will probably be. In one church where I taught for seven years, four sheets of A4 paper were generally enough. If I wrote more than four pages I began wondering if I could teach the whole message in one session. If you find you have more material than usual, think about cutting the message into two parts, and then refocus your effort on finishing the first half.

Get familiar with your notes. Rehearse them a couple of times. This isn't in order to make you a performer, but it does help you to be familiar with your message. When you know the structure of your message you won't get ahead of yourself and find you left out some important point. Trying to fit that point in might break up your line of logic and confuse your listeners. As you read over your notes you might discover something that reads okay but it isn't the way you would say it. You can to rewrite it to make it your natural expression.

If necessary, make notes in the margin of your notes in red, note transition places, make notes to yourself: "read verses 3–7 here".

Make your notes serve your needs. They don't have to be like anyone else's. You won't teach like anyone else.

Rob's method

I use a large print Bible to teach from. It's legible on the pulpit desk! I used to write little tiny notes on one sheet of paper because my pastor showed me his notes, and I thought that's how it was supposed to be done. Later on I thought, "Why do I have to do that? I can't read my notes! I ought to make my notes work for me, not against me!"

I use half sheets of A5 scrap paper (that makes it A5 size, 5 1/5" x 8 1/2"). That size fits into my teaching Bible, making the notes less obvious than big sheets of paper. I use scrap paper, because if I'm stuck, I can throw paper away and start fresh, or I can cut off the part that works and staple it onto a new sheet and keep working.

The notebook holes are already punched in the paper so I won't write over holes and lose words when I put the notes into my ring binder later. I save everything I do: I have worked too hard to just throw it away. I might use a message again if I teach somewhere else. I will write a note to myself on the first page if I think God blessed the message. If God blessed it once, He will probably bless it again if I believe He is leading me to teach it. I also note which messages, in my opinion, didn't go well.

I use a combination of outlining and write-it-out-in-full. The outlining helps me to structure the message in a logical progression of thoughts. I write out fully what I want to say; points are then thought out, my transitions flow smoothly, I know how I want to express myself instead of trying to figure out on the spot what I am trying to say. I want to use whatever God might give me as I teach, like a word of knowledge, a word of wisdom, or a prophecy, but I still have a solid message if God doesn't add to it, and I still know where I'm going after I give that spontaneous word from God.

I make sure I book mark in my Bible Scriptures I want to quote during the message (if I don't write them out in my notes). I don't want to have to look them up as I teach.

I believe that God will anoint me as I study, and anoint me as I teach.

8. Make it your habit to grow

It can be overwhelming to think about teaching through the whole Bible. You need depth and experience. You need to understand the Bible. How will you get that? I often thought: Wouldn't it be great to start ministering as a 60-year old teacher who has been doing it for 40 years?

There is no instant way to approach teaching the Bible. But you can grow into it.

God has designed life so that we are born small and must grow and develop. Part of the growth comes from God, part of it comes from us. God gives life and potential; we practice and learn and grow. As we practice skills of teaching, we will get better at it.

Teaching is a gift from the Holy Spirit that He gives as He chooses to whom He wills. Either you have that gift or you don't. The ministry is not something we choose. He chooses us. How do you know you have the gift? Because you do it naturally. It's the way God created you to be. You have an ability to make someone learn something. You have the patience to work with someone until they get it. You have joy when they grasp the concept and begin to act on it. You will also have the desire to learn. My pastor said once that if you have the gift of teaching, you will have the gift of studying as well. They go together. If you hate to study and learn, it wouldn't make sense for God to make you a teacher.

God wants us to grow and develop by using what He gives. He gives us muscles in our body. We can cause them to grow by using them. The reverse is also true: we can waste those muscles because we don't use them. Anything we have will either grow because we use it, or waste away because we don't use it.

God gives us tremendous potential: life, our minds, our bodies, His Holy Spirit to empower us. Then we make that potential into reality: we live and practice and develop and grow.

As we do this, we are developing our lives. Our lives are part of the teaching ministry. Our teaching comes from our lives. What we say has to be the same as how we live, otherwise we are saying one thing with our mouths and something else with our lives. Therefore we must prepare our lives to teach as much as we prepare our messages.

Here are things we can do to make sure we grow.

Read to become familiar with the Bible

It's so simple that we might miss this: read the Bible every day for the rest of your life. The more you read, the more familiar you become with it. The more you know it, the easier the Holy Spirit can connect things together to teach you.

Read to become more familiar, not necessarily to understand it. People think they have to understand what they read, and they stop when they are puzzled. Instead, read on and don't worry if you don't understand it. Understanding will come later, and you can also prepare to grow in that as well. But what you need is to become familiar with the whole Bible, even with the places you don't understand. At least you will be familiar with the questions.

Have a system of reading. Make it something you do every day. As you persevere in this, you will become very familiar with the Bible. It will greatly benefit your life, which will then benefit your teaching.

What kind of system depends on what kind of person you are. People are different. Some are very systematic, others are not. David couldn't use Saul's armour. He made war against Goliath, but he had to do it his way. These are not hard and fast commandments. Experiment with these suggestions to see what works for you.

I say this because I have tried out all kinds of systems, and none of them really worked for me. For example, I tried reading the Bible in a year, but I would get behind and be off schedule. That was discouraging.

What works for me is very simple. I read the New Testament in the morning when I get up. I read the Old Testament in the evening before I go to bed. That way I am in both parts of the Bible at the same time. The Holy Spirit can connect something I read in the morning with something I read at night, or the other way around. I keep bookmarks where I read, and I can pick up from where I left off. When I finish Revelation, the very next morning I am in Matthew. When I finish Malachi, the very next night I begin Genesis again.

If you use this system and read three chapters in the morning and three in the evening, you would read the Old Testament twice in a year, and the New Testament three times in a year. If you did that for ten years, you would have read the Old Testament twenty times, and the New Testament thirty times. Do you think you would be more familiar with the Bible at that point?

If you already have a reading system, persevere in it! If you don't have a system, try this one and adapt it so it fits who you are. For example, my wife found that when she read the Old Testament at night she would go to sleep almost immediately. That bothered her. So she switched it around so that she read OT in the morning when she was more awake, and the NT at night. I don't think it matters how we do this, as long as we do it. Play with a system until you discover how you can regularly read the Bible.

Make up your mind to become familiar with the Bible. The journey of a thousand miles begins with the first step. As you get familiar with the Bible, you will grow in your life and in your teaching.

Study to grow in knowledge

You grow in knowledge by taking time to study Scripture. Here is where you take time to read carefully, ask questions of the text, look up words, use reference books, get the answer to the question you are asking. The more you learn, the more you can grow in your own life, and in your teaching.

Study tools can be: a dictionary in your own language, a concordance for your Bible, a Bible dictionary, an encyclopaedia. For me, the dictionary is really helpful. Teachers communicate ideas. We use words to do this. If we don't know what a word means, we can't communicate the idea. We also have to help others learn the words so they can understand. People can't think right without the right vocabulary. So part of our job is using the right words and making sure people get the right idea when we use that word. The people who write dictionaries work hard to clearly and sharply define a word. They point out synonyms, words that are similar in meaning, and they also show the shade of difference in meaning between those synonyms. Dictionaries do a lot of our work for us. If you use a dictionary app, you can look over many words quickly.

Even though I knew I was called to teach the Bible, I didn't know how to study it. My own natural ability was not enough. I needed to grow but didn't know how. That's when I found *Living by the Book* by Howard Hendricks and William Hendricks. Howard taught Bible study forty years at Dallas Theological Seminary before he wrote the book. It is the best book you can get to learn how to study the Bible. Go get it! Then you can share my book with someone who wants to know how to get started but might be intimidated if you gave them Hendricks.

Meditate to grow in understanding

Meditating is thinking deeply about something in order to understand it. It is the final step in the process of taking in the Bible.

Meditating is like digesting our food. We put food into our mouths, we chew it, we enjoy the taste. Then we swallow and it goes into our stomach, where acids and enzymes take the food apart into glucose (sugar), fats, amino acids (proteins), vitamins. Then those components are absorbed into our bodies (amino acids become proteins, fat gets stored, simple sugar becomes our fuel, minerals are taken into our bones), and the waste products are eliminated. What we eat becomes part of us.

Reading the Bible and studying it is like taking food into our bodies. We take the sentences apart into words and look them up and make sure we learn what the words are saying. It's like chewing up food. Then we meditate—it's like digestion, receiving the words of God and making them part of our lives, our thoughts, our emotions, our wills, and our choices.

If we don't meditate it's like chewing up our food and then spitting it out. What will happen to us if we do that?

Meditation is so important that we will consider it on its own in the next chapter.

Pray to have fellowship with God

I feel inadequate to write about this because I don't think I'm a great person of prayer. But I am convinced that prayer is necessary, and I have given more effort to pray than ever before.

This is one of those areas that I have not found much help from books, though I read every book on prayer that I have and look for others. I think there is a great spiritual opposition to prayer. The devil does not want us to pray, and one reason for this is that it will damage us personally if we do not pray. We lose out on being with God and receiving His life, His wisdom, His peace, His perspective on life and the ministry. We are the losers if we don't pray. Our lack of prayer will also hurt others, slow God's work down, and ultimately open opportunities up for the devil to work against God.

If we do pray the devil is damaged, his work is damaged, people are set free and transformed, and the kingdom of God is advanced.

After a long time of trying to pray, I found a great definition of prayer while reading The Living Bible. I was reading Daniel 6, and in verses 10–11 it says, "But though Daniel knew about it, he went home and knelt down as usual in his upstairs bedroom, with its windows open toward Jerusalem, and prayed three times a day, just as he always had, giving thanks to his God. Then the men thronged to Daniel's house and found him praying there, asking favors of his God."

I saw that for Daniel prayer wasn't complicated. It was *giving thanks* and *asking favours* of God.

Thanksgiving and praise keeps us safe

When someone does something good for you, it is right to acknowledge that with thanks. When you do not acknowledge a good done for you, it is an insult to the one who did good.

If that is so with men, it is more so with God. Remember that God made everything good. God's goodness is all around us. Are we aware of His goodness and acknowledging it with thanks?

This is one of the first steps away from God, as Paul said in Romans 1:20–21, "For since the creation of the world His invisible attributes are clearly seen, being understood by the things that are made, even His eternal power and His Godhead, so they are without excuse, because, although they knew God, they did not glorify Him as God, nor were thankful, but became futile in their thoughts, and their foolish hearts were darkened."

We want to be careful to give God thanks regularly because it is extremely ungodly to not give thanks to God. Unthankfulness is the first step away from God, just as thankfulness is the first step towards God: "Enter into His courts with thanksgiving, and into His courts with praise" (Psalm 100:4).

When we think about what to give thanks for, we can thank God for anything and everything, even the things we don't like or think are good. That's what Paul says in Ephesians 5:20, "...giving thanks always for all things to God the Father in the name of our Lord Jesus Christ."

It might seem like we are crazy to give God thanks for things that we don't approve of. I tried it once, though. I was really frustrated about my ministry, and could only think of what was going wrong. I was convicted by my lack of prayer and decided to begin praying by giving thanks. I thought to myself, "Give thanks? For what?!" I remembered the above Scripture in Ephesians 5 and thanked God for everything that I thought was going wrong. I felt all the tension drain from my body. I had peace.

It took me a while to figure out how I could thank God and have peace over things that I wasn't happy with. I read later: "And we know that all things work together for good to those who love God, to those who are the called according to His purpose" (Romans 8:28). I realized that God is able to make the good things work out for good, and He is also able to make all the nasty, stinky, rotten things work out for good. I can thank God for that thing that I don't like because God will work it out for good, and I don't have to know how. I can thank Him now in faith. I can thank God for all things and have peace because He is good and will work all things together for good.

Thanksgiving has become important for me so that I keep my perspective on life. Otherwise I am not seeing God in everything. I am missing what God is doing. I am practicing to be an atheist. I want to make sure that I am noticing what good things God is doing and give thanks for that.

I also tell my prayer group to deliberately spend time in thanking God each time we get together. We don't want to rush into asking for things, important and good as that is. First, we want to remember all the good things God is doing and acknowledge them as much as we can.

Then we want to ask favours of God

Once we have given thanks, then let's ask favours of God. Let's ask for His will to be accomplished on earth as it is in heaven.

We will ask with much more faith, trusting in His great goodness, knowing that God is "able to do exceedingly abundantly above all that we ask or think, according to the power that works in us (Ephesians 3:20)."

That's what Daniel asked for, favours from God. A favour is an act of kindness beyond what is due or usual, as in: "I've come to ask you a favour." We don't deserve anything from God. His gifts all come from His grace. So it comes down to this: what does God want to do? That's what I want to ask for. So I pray that the Holy Spirit guides me in my prayers to ask for what God wants to do. That's where I begin to practice saying not what I will, but what You will.

> Heavenly Father, I want to confess that it's easier to do anything else than pray. I'm sorry that there is something deep inside me that doesn't want You. I can't be spiritual without You. Please work in me to love You with all my heart, soul, and strength, and help me to pray. In Jesus' name, amen.

The next chapter talks about a great help to prayer.

9. Meditating in the Bible

Meditation is so important that we want to consider it apart from reading, studying, and praying. This is something God has made so that we can grow in knowing Him and grow in our life with Him. The difference in life with and without meditation is beyond day and night, it is literally life and death.

The main idea behind meditation is this: what is produced from our lives comes as a result of what we put into our lives. As we take God's truth into us, our lives will be transformed, be made successful, and partake of eternal life. Do you want to know more about this? It's all there in Psalm 1.

1 Blessed is the man who walks not in the counsel of the ungodly, nor stands in the path of sinners, nor sits in the seat of the scornful;

2 But his delight is in the law of the Lord, and in His law he meditates day and night.

3 He shall be like a tree planted by the rivers of water, that brings forth its fruit in its season, whose leaf also shall not wither; and whatever he does shall prosper.

4 The ungodly are not so, but are like the chaff which the wind drives away.

5 Therefore the ungodly shall not stand in the judgment, nor sinners in the congregation of the righteous.

6 For the Lord knows the way of the righteous, but the way of the ungodly shall perish.

Blessed is the man

This psalm is about being happy. That's what the word translated "blessed" means in the original Hebrew language.

There is the kind of happiness that comes when things turn out right. That happiness is based on circumstances. An example might be, I won the lottery, I'm happy, because I have a lot of money. Or, my money got stolen, now I'm unhappy.

The translators chose the word "blessed" because it does not depend on circumstances, but on God's power to cause all things to work out together for good. As we said before, that means all the things we would think of as "good" and all the things we would think of as "bad". God makes all things work together for good, which means we can't lose. It will all be good. God says so.

But it is possible to live as if there were other equally valid ways to make ourselves happy, and thus ignore the God of the Bible. Ungodly people go this way. And they encourage all people to think the same way, to live as if there were other gods, other ways to make ourselves happy.

Psalm 1 says any other way does not work. The other ways promise happiness, but end in disappointment.

When you follow the counsel of the ungodly (which is, be happy your own way, without the God of the Bible), you come into the path of sinners, those who are going the wrong way. And it ends in sitting in the seat of the scornful, those who pridefully despise others. That becomes a dead end.

One thing that is not found in the way of the ungodly is satisfaction. There is no peace for the wicked, nor is there delight or joy. The promises to the ungodly are not fulfilled. They turn out to be lies. There is only disappointment, not satisfaction. That way leads away from light, from life, from true happiness.

But his delight is in the law of the LORD

But the one who listens to the law of the Lord has delight. That's because the Word of the Lord is true. The promises of God are fulfilled. He cannot lie. Therefore there is real satisfaction and joy and peace for the one who listens to the law of the Lord. That person is going the right way, and will end up in the right place.

And in His law he meditates day and night

The one who listens to the law of the Lord fills himself with it and thinks about it all the time. And at the same time he does not listen to the wicked when they speak about happiness in any other way than the God of the Bible. He fills himself with the one and rejects the other.

It would be a strange position to listen to God in some things and to the devil in others. That's like eating food with poison in it and saying, "Well, most of it is not bad." We can't go two ways at once. If we are going to go God's way, then we want to go His way all the way in every respect.

The root of His way is to be filled with the Word of God.

Then Jesus said to those Jews who believed Him, "If you abide in My word, you are My disciples indeed." John 8:31

"If you abide in Me, and My words abide in you, you will ask what you desire, and it shall be done for you." John 15:7

Therefore let that abide in you which you heard from the beginning. If what you heard from the beginning abides in you, you also will abide in the Son and in the Father. 1 John 2:24

Let the word of Christ dwell in you richly in all wisdom, teaching and admonishing one another in psalms and hymns and spiritual songs, singing with grace in your hearts to the Lord. Colossians 3:16

Blessings of meditation

Now we are going to see what are the results of being filled with the Word of God.

He shall be like a tree. I never knew anyone ever wish to be a tree! So what is so important about being a tree? It depends on what you are right now.

The voice said, "Cry out!" And he said, "What shall I cry?" "All flesh is grass, and all its loveliness is like the flower of the field. The grass withers, the flower fades, because the breath of the LORD blows upon it; surely the people are grass. The grass withers, the flower fades, but the word of our God stands forever." Isaiah 40:6–8

All flesh is grass. Not permanent, not strong. Here today, gone tomorrow.

But the one who meditates becomes like a tree. That means strong, planted deep, long life, bearing fruit, things that grass can't do or be.

What does it take to change grass into a tree? You have to transform it completely from the inside out. Man cannot do this, but God can.

And do not be conformed to this world, but be transformed by the renewing of your mind, that you may prove what is that good and acceptable and perfect will of God. Romans 12:2

We renew our minds when we meditate on the Word of God. We are transformed from being those who don't believe God into those who do believe God, and who see God work for them.

Planted by rivers of water. Planted means more than just a tree stuck in the dirt. It means having a superabundant supply for the tree. A tree needs soil. It is planted in plenty of soil, a whole planet, if need be. A tree needs carbon dioxide. There is a global atmosphere of carbon dioxide more than enough for the tree. A tree needs sunlight. The sun produces way more than the tree will ever need. A tree needs water. This verse says there are rivers, not just one, but a superabundance of water for the tree.

Water is a symbol for the Holy Spirit in the Bible. Jesus spoke about this.

> On the last day, that great day of the feast, Jesus stood and cried out, saying, "If anyone thirsts, let him come to Me and drink. He who believes in Me, as the Scripture has said, out of his heart will flow rivers of living water." But this He spoke concerning the Spirit, whom those believing in Him would receive; for the Holy Spirit was not yet given, because Jesus was not yet glorified. John 7:37–39

Have you ever wondered how the Holy Spirit would ever flow out of your heart? When you fill yourself with the Word of God, He will.

> "It is the Spirit who gives life; the flesh profits nothing. The words that I speak to you are spirit, and they are life." John 6:63
> For the word of God is living and powerful, and sharper than any two-edged sword, piercing even to the division of soul and spirit, and of joints and marrow, and is a discerner of the thoughts and intents of the heart. Hebrews 4:12
> ... having been born again, not of corruptible seed but incorruptible, through the word of God which lives and abides forever. 1 Peter 1:23

Trees are living water pumps. They can pump as much as 300 gallons of water out of their leaves in a day. But it is water vapour, gentle and refreshing, not like a fire hose that could knock a person down with its force. As you meditate and fill your life with the Word of God, you too will experience the gentle refreshing of the Holy Spirit in your life, and others will as well.

Bears fruit in its season. We all want to bear fruit for Jesus. It says here that when we meditate in the Word of the Lord, we will naturally bear fruit. Notice that fruit is for others, not for the tree. A tree does not eat its own fruit. This means we will be able to give of ourselves to others and not be exhausted. We learn that whatever we receive from the Lord, there is always more where that came from.

Leaf shall not wither. Trees get their energy direct from the heavens. With their leaves they make the sunlight into starch for its food. There is plenty of sun to use. And the leaves will not wither. The tree that we will be is an evergreen tree. We will always be able to receive all that we need from the Lord.

Whatever he does shall prosper. Here the psalmist has left talking about trees. He is saying that everything a meditator does will be successful. Is that promising too much?

The reason why a meditator will be successful is that he is meditating on the will of God. What we meditate upon, this we do. This is what God commanded Joshua:

> "Be strong and of good courage, for to this people you shall divide as an inheritance the land which I swore to their fathers to give them. Only be strong and very courageous, that you may observe to do according to all the law which Moses My servant commanded you; do not turn from it to the right hand or to the left, that you may prosper wherever you go. This Book of the Law shall

not depart from your mouth, but you shall meditate in it day and night, that you may observe to do according to all that is written in it. For then you will make your way prosperous, and then you will have good success."
Joshua 1:6–8

God called Joshua to do something that not even Moses could do: bring Israel into the Promised Land.

The way God told Joshua to accomplish it was to observe the law of Moses.

In order to observe the law of Moses, Joshua was to meditate in that law day and night. Then he would do the law, and then he would be successful.

So the biblical way to live is to meditate on the will of God, then we will do His will, and then we will be successful in all that we do, because we trust God to establish His will. If we are not obeying God, that means we are not meditating on His word. We are not filling ourselves with His Word. So this is where we must correct ourselves.

God is very interested in establishing His will. As we do what He wants, He will work through us.

This is the true word of faith, the true way that God makes us successful: as we meditate on His Word, and live according to it.

Warnings of meditation

The psalmist goes on to say what will happen if a man does not meditate in God's Word.

The ungodly are like chaff. Chaff is the outer part of a seed of wheat. It has to be removed in order to be ground and made into flour. It can't be eaten; it's no good for anything. It is lighter than the seed and is easily blown away; it used to be alive but is dead, and it is easily burned.

People not receiving life from God are outwardly alive for now, but they have no inner life. When the wind of judgment comes, they will truly be separated from God forever.

Neither the ungodly nor sinners shall stand. We understand the first part: of course the ungodly will not stand in the future judgment. But they won't stand in the congregation of the righteous at the present either. The reason is that the righteous are those who receive life from God, and they receive it through being in His Word. They are able to give because they bear fruit in season. The whole church is able to give to one another in love. The body of Christ serves one another and builds one another up. If someone who is an unbeliever comes into the church there will be a great difference. He won't be able to give. He has no connection with God. So unbelievers take life, they don't give life. As it says in 1 John 3:14–16:

> We know that we have passed from death to life, because we love the brethren. He who does not love his brother abides in death. Whoever hates his brother is a murderer, and you know that no murderer has eternal life abiding in him. By this we know love, because He laid down His life for us. And we also ought to lay down our lives for the brethren.

A murderer is someone who takes life. He can take life quickly, with a knife or a gun. A murderer can also take life slowly, a bit at a time, just by demanding his own way. It takes a lot longer to kill this way, but it does kill.

A taker will be very noticeable in a church of givers. After a while the church begins to notice that a so-called brother is borrowing money, trying to be romantic with the sisters, causes arguments, and just doesn't act like someone who has been born again. It becomes obvious over time. A person can talk like a Christian and say all the right things, but it is hard to fake living like a Christian because a Christian can lay down his life for the brethren, and an unbeliever can't. He only knows how to take life, whether slow or fast. Either he has to repent and believe in Jesus, or else he has to leave the church.

A healthy church should be able to discern wolves and those pretending to be believers and make it so they can't stay in the church in peace. Ananias and Sapphira should not be able to live unnoticed in our congregations.

Call for decision

The end of Psalm 1 ends with a contrast. The way of the ungodly will perish. It is a dead end. God will not allow those who deny Him to keep at it while He keeps them alive. Everybody gets to have their own way for a while. Then God will end the way of the ungodly.

The Lord knows the way of the righteous. That goes beyond a simple knowing of what they are doing and where they are going. It means God is intimately involved in the lives of His people. They are on His way, and He understands their steps, even if they don't. He is there from the beginning, and He will lead them safely to the end.

Here we have life and death. It is life to live with God and know Him. Jesus said, "And this is eternal life, that they may know You, the only true God, and Jesus Christ whom You have sent (John 17:3)."

It is death to live apart from God. It can only end with complete loss, as Jesus says in Mark 8:36:

> "For what will it profit a man if he gains the whole world, and loses his own soul?"

Which do you choose? What do you want to be, grass or a tree? If you want to be grass, you don't have to do anything.

If you want to be a tree, then you have something to do: reject the counsel of the ungodly and meditate in the Word of God day and night.

Everything else comes out of that.

How to meditate in the Word of God

When we read, we can take a lot of Scripture, and we don't have to worry about understanding. When we meditate, we take a small part of Scripture and focus on understanding. That's what meditation is about.

Pick a book. The first step in meditating is to pick a book of the Bible to meditate in. The bad news is that the Bible is so big, you probably won't have enough time to meditate through it all. The good news is you can meditate through some of it, so find a part to meditate in, and do that. Start with the first verse, and meditate through the book to the end. When you finish that book, do another. Pray and ask God what would be His choice of book for you. Take the first thing that He gives you and do that. I began in Proverbs. I thought that would take forever to go through one verse at a time. It only took ten years, but that was because I quit so many times. Every time I began again to meditate, I had to go back to where I left off. I learned to not quit and keep going even when it was so slow. I also learned how to study, because I had to learn what each proverb meant before I could meditate on it. So I learned to study and look up words. As I practiced I found it got easier to do. I was learning! I found that I was learning how to study and teach the Bible. It was like God was teaching me, and I was in His school. So pray, ask God where He wants you to meditate, and pick a book of the Bible.

Take time. The second step is to take time to do this. Some people like doing this in the morning, others late in the day, some in the night. Find what works best for you. It helps when it is quiet and there are no distractions.

God says to meditate day and night, which means all the time. The goal is to be consistent. Just like we eat for our bodies, we want to eat for our souls.

Pray, read the context, look up words, write it down. The third step is to pray and ask God to bless your meditating time and teach you.

Then begin thinking about the verse that you are on. Ask questions like you do when you study. I spend time reading it over and over. I read the paragraph so I do not lose the context. If I have more questions I look them up. I think about other Scriptures as they come to mind.

I write things down to help myself think. In *Lectures to My Students* chapter ten Charles Spurgeon quotes M. Bautain: "Now this analysis of the idea, which displays it, as it were, before the eyes of the mind, is well executed only by writing. The pen is the scalpel which dissects the thoughts." I have learned that as I write my thoughts out, even if it's only half a thought, the rest of the thought comes as I write.

Meditate until you have a response to God. I stay with a verse as long as it takes to understand it. It can be frustrating to spend a lot of time on a verse, but if I am patient, I can learn a lot. I remember meditating on the idea of "good". I looked up the word in the dictionary, and it didn't help because it was feeble and uninspiring. I thought, "The dictionary is failing me! Stupid dictionary." Then I asked God, "What does 'good' mean?" I was out of time, so I left it for the day and went on to my work.

The next day, I asked God again, "Please teach me what 'good' means." I thought I should look up the first place in the Bible where the word was used. I was so surprised! It is used seven times in the very first chapter in Genesis. Everything God made was good. I started thinking about how God is good, and everything He made has His goodness built into it. I saw God's goodness in the sky, in the trees, in the air that I breathe, everywhere I looked. I began to thank God and worship Him because He is good and gives good to us. I wrote it down so I would not forget. When I think about that now, I want to thank God all over again that He is so good. I'm so glad I got to grow a little bit through that meditation.

I know I have meditated through a verse when I have a response to God. Sometimes when I realize what a verse means I respond to God with worship and thanks and praise. I am growing in my worship and ability to rejoice in God.

Sometimes I realize that I am not doing what the verse says, or I am disobeying God. I confess my sin to God and ask for cleansing by the blood of Jesus. That strengthens my relationship to God, it humbles me, and I learn to hate my sin more and trust Jesus more.

Sometimes I am reminded of a person who needs what I have meditated upon, and I pray that God would bless them in that way. Now I am interceding in prayer for others.

In each case, I respond to God in prayer. I am practicing my relationship with God and growing in faith and understanding. I am being transformed in my thoughts because I am not thinking my way but God's way. Prayer becomes natural because it comes as a result.

Do it every day. Psalm 1 says to take time every day and meditate. Start with a little time each day, and work up to longer times as you are able. Doing it every day works to discipline us. We learn to say no to distractions and concentrate on saying yes to God.

When you start to do this, expect the devil to throw distractions your way. You might watch all kinds of things go wrong. This means you are on the right way. When I am reminded of all the tasks I need to do right away, I just write them down so I don't forget, say thank you to the devil for reminding me, and keep meditating.

As we persevere in this we will have a good harvest. We are planting the good seed of the Word of God in us. We can expect to have a harvest of righteousness thirty, sixty, and even a hundred times what we sowed. If we plant evil in us, we can expect thirty, sixty, and a hundred-fold harvest of judgment. If we plant something neither good nor bad in us, just "*bleah*", we will have a harvest of thirty, sixty, or a hundred-fold "*bleah*" in our lives. I can't afford a life full of nothing!

We are always sowing into our lives. There isn't a time when we are not putting things into our minds. Therefore, we must take care what we plant. We sow, looking ahead to what we will reap.

Teach others how to do it. I think you will find meditating helpful. My own experience is that I could not live without it. If you find this helpful, teach others how to do it. When people are filling themselves with the Word of God, there is no limit to what God will do with them. Man is able to count the seeds in a fruit. Only God can count the number of fruit in a seed.

Expect God to bless your sowing and reaping in Jesus' name.

10. Summary

When I was starting out as a Bible teacher, I really needed help to learn to teach. I never went to Bible college or seminary. I listened to my pastor teach for years. Then I found myself in the position of a pastor, and I had to teach the Bible. I had a gift from the Holy Spirit to teach, and I enjoyed it, but I found out quickly it was hard work. It demanded more from me than I knew. I needed to grow in my ability to study and observe. I needed to grow as a person. I needed a method and a way to approach the Scriptures to feed the people week after week, and I didn't have one.

The first person I found help from was Anne Graham Lotz in a book on evangelism. Here is what she said.

> Keep in mind three questions that you will ask yourself as you go through the Scriptures.
>
> First, "What does the passage say? What is the content of the passage?" And in this particular aspect of your study, be as literal as you can. Just summarize the facts in the passage, don't spiritualize, don't get into personal applications, just summarize the facts. Try to keep your summary to one sentence. And that makes you brief, specific, and factual. Think of what is the subject of the passage, what they are saying, what they are doing, where are they going, what's happening. Put that into your sentence that describes the content of the passage.

Second, you need to ask yourself, "What should a Christian get out of this passage? What's the spiritual lesson to be learned?" To find the spiritual lesson, you might ask yourself, "What are the people in the passage doing, not doing that they should be doing, or doing that they should not be doing?" Put yourself in and try to draw the spiritual lesson from it.

Now we come to the applications. These can be tough for Christians who are used to being spoon-fed, who are used to studying the Scriptures as something precious and holy, but are not something to take into their lives. Take out the spiritual lesson from the passage and put it in the form of a question, and ask it to yourself. Ask what God would have you do in response to that passage. Is there an example for me to follow? Is there a sin to avoid? Is there a promise to claim? Is there a prayer to repeat? Is there a command to obey? Is there a condition to meet? Is there a verse to memorize? Is there an error to mark? Is there a challenge to face?

Put yourself into the passage and you bring it home.[1]

The Bible already has the message in it that every person needs to hear. All we want to do is accurately get the message out and accurately deliver it. May the Lord of the harvest send out more labourers into His harvest.

You therefore, my son, be strong in the grace that is in Christ Jesus. And the things that you have heard from me among many witnesses, commit these to faithful men who will be able to teach others also. 2 Timothy 2:1–2

---

1 The Work of an Evangelist, (Minneapolis: World Wide Publications, 1984), p. 272–273

Prayer

Thank You, Heavenly Father, that we are Yours, that You call us, You equip us, You send us. Help us to live with You, growing in You, knowing You. Please fill us with Your Holy Spirit. Make us strong and able by Your grace. Help us to teach others. We commit ourselves to You.

We pray in Jesus' name. Amen.

About the author

Rob Dingman came to Christ slowly but surely by 1974. He began serving Jesus by playing in Christian rock ministry bands. He and his wife Joanie spent a year in Japan with the Robert Case Band, then they moved to Germany and helped establish Calvary Chapel Siegen in 1990. They have lived in United Kingdom since 1997, helping to establish churches and teaching people how to study and meditate in the Bible.

They have two daughters, Holly and Katie.

Rob is available for seminars and conferences. He has teaching videos on Vimeo and YouTube.

Contact him at www.calvarychapeltwickenham.com.

CPSIA information can be obtained
at www.ICGtesting.com
Printed in the USA
FFOW03n0929170117
31437FF